William Fairfield Warren

**The True Key to ancient Cosmology and Mythical Geography**

William Fairfield Warren

**The True Key to ancient Cosmology and Mythical Geography**

ISBN/EAN: 9783337191306

Printed in Europe, USA, Canada, Australia, Japan

Cover: Foto ©ninafisch / pixelio.de

More available books at **www.hansebooks.com**

# THE TRUE KEY

TO

# ANCIENT COSMOLOGY

AND

# MYTHICAL GEOGRAPHY.

BY

WILLIAM F. WARREN, S.T.D., LL.D.,

*President of Boston University; Author of "Anfangsgründe der Lôgik,"*
*"Einleitung in die systematische Theologie," etc.*

THIRD EDITION. ILLUSTRATED.

BOSTON
PUBLISHED BY GINN, HEATH, & CO.
1882.

TO

My Honored Colleague and Friend,

# BORDEN P. BOWNE, LL.D.,

RESPECTFULLY INSCRIBED.

# PREFACE TO THE THIRD EDITION.

———————◆———————

THE suggestion that the true cosmology of Homer has for more than four hundred years eluded the research of scholars, is hardly less startling and paradoxical than was in its time the great thesis of Copernicus. Nevertheless, as the Key here presented clearly shows, —

"It is not Homer nods, but we that dream."

Since the paper first appeared, no critic has publicly challenged its correctness. Meantime in private correspondence several of the most distinguished and specially competent scholars of Europe, such as Mr. Gladstone, Professor Sayce of Oxford, and Professor Tiele of Leyden, have frankly indicated their favorable inclination of judgment toward it.

During the past winter the author delivered in the post-graduate department of the University an extended course of lectures on the Comparative Cosmology and Mythical Geography of the Most Ancient Nations. The class consisted of eighteen men, and all problems raised in the free discussions connected with the course found ready and satisfactory answers in accordance with the principles here set forth.

The first publication of this Key was in "The Independent,"

5

New York, Aug. 25, 1881. The second and enlarged issue
was in the "Boston University Year Bóok," Vol. IX. The
present, or third, edition is the first in independent form, and is
illustrated not only with the original diagram, but also with a
wood-cut view of "The World of the Ancients" reconstructed
according to the Key here presented.

W. F. W.

Boston, April, 1882.

# THE TRUE KEY TO ANCIENT COSMOLOGY AND MYTHICAL GEOGRAPHY.

*Hic vertex nobis semper sublimis, at illum*
*Sub pedibus Styx atra videt Manesque profundi.*

THE cosmology of the ancients has been gravely misconceived by modern scholars. All our maps of "The World according to Homer" represent the earth as flat, and as surrounded by a level, flowing, ocean stream. "There can be no doubt," says Bunbury, "that Homer, in common with all his successors down to the time of Hecatæus, believed the earth to be a plane of circular form."[1] As to the sky, we are generally taught that the early Greeks believed it to be a solid metallic vault.[2] Professor F. A. Paley aids the imagination of his readers as follows: "We might familiarly illustrate the Hesiodic notion of the flat circular earth and the convex overarching sky by a circular plate with a hemispherical dish-cover of metal placed over it and concealing it. Above

---

[1] E. H. Bunbury, *History of Ancient Geography among the Greeks and Romans.* London, 1879: vol. i., p. 79. Professor Bunbury was a leading contributor to Smith's *Dictionary of Ancient Greek and Roman Geography.* Compare Friedreich, *Die Realien in der Ilids und Odysee.* 1856, § 19. Buchholz, *Die homerische Realien.* Leipzig, 1871: Bd. I., 48.

[2] See Voss, Ukert, Bunbury, Buchholz, and the others.

the cover (which is supposed to rotate on an axis, πόλος)
live the gods. Round the inner concavity is the path of
the sun, giving light to the earth below."[1]

That all writers upon Greek mythology, including even
the latest,[2] should proceed upon the same assumptions
as the professed Homeric interpreters and geographers,
building upon their foundations, is only natural. And
that the current conceptions of the cosmology of the
ancient Greeks should profoundly affect current interpre-
tations of the cosmological and geographical data of other
ancient peoples, is also precisely what the history and inner
relationships of modern archæological studies would lead
one to expect. It is not surprising, therefore, that the
earth of the ancient Hebrews, Egyptians, Indo-Aryans,
and other ancient peoples, has been assumed to correspond
to the supposed flat earth of the Greeks.[3]

A protracted study of the subject has convinced the
present writer that this modern assumption, as to the form
of the Homeric earth, is entirely baseless and misleading.
He has, furthermore, satisfied himself that the Egyptians,
Akkadians, Assyrians, Babylonians, Phœnicians, Hebrews,

---

[1] *The Epics of Hesiod, with an English Commentary.* London, 1861: p. 172.

[2] See, for example, Sir George W. Cox: *An Introduction to the Science
of Comparative Mythology and Folklore.* London and New York, 1881: p.
244. Decharme, *Mythologie de la Grèce Antique.* Paris, 1879: p. 11.

[3] It is true that Heinrich Zimmer remarks, "Die Anschauung die sich
bei Griechen und Nordgermanen findet, dass die Erde eine Scheibe sei,
um die sich das Meer schlingt, begegnet in den vedischen Samhitā nir-
gends." *Altindisches Leben.* Berlin, 1879: p. 359. But even he does not
advance from this negative assertion to an exposition of the true Vedic
cosmology. Compare M. Fontane: "Leur cosmographie est embryonaire.
La terre est pour l'Arya ronde et plate comme un disque. Le firmament
védique, concave, vien se souder à la terre, circulairement, à l'horizon."
*Inde Védique.* Paris, 1881: p. 94.

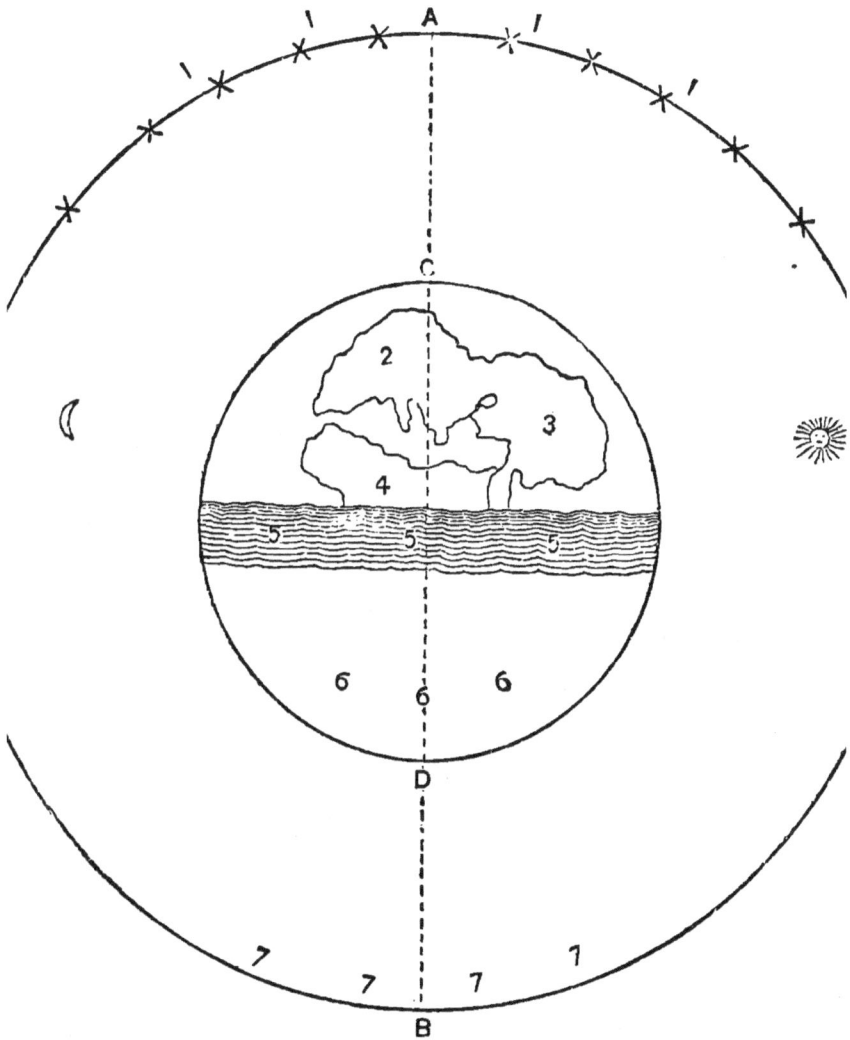

Greeks, Iranians, Indo-Aryans, Chinese, Japanese, — in fine,
all the most ancient historic peoples, — possessed in their
earliest traceable periods a cosmology essentially identical,
and one of a far more advanced type than has been attrib-
uted to them. The purpose of this paper is to set forth

and illustrate this oldest known conception of the universe and of its parts.

In ancient thought the grand divisions of the world are four; to wit, The abode of the gods, the abode of living men, the abode of the dead, and, finally, the abode of demons. To locate these in right mutual relations, one must begin by representing to himself the earth as a sphere or spheroid, and as situated within, and concentric with, the starry sphere, *each having its axis perpendicular, and its north pole at the top.* The pole-star is thus in the true zenith, and the heavenly heights centring about it are the abode of the supreme god or gods. According to the same conception, the upper or northern hemisphere of the earth is the proper home of living men; the under or southern hemisphere of the earth, the abode of disembodied spirits and rulers of the dead; and, finally, the undermost region of all, that centring around the southern pole of the heavens, the lowest hell. The two hemispheres of the earth were furthermore conceived of as separated from each other by an equatorial ocean or oceanic current.

To illustrate this conception of the world, let the two circles of the diagram upon the preceding page represent respectively the earth-sphere and the outermost of the revolving starry spheres. A is the north pole of the heavens, so placed as to be in the zenith. B is the south pole of the heavens, in the nadir. The line A B is the axis of the apparent revolution of the starry heavens in a perpendicular position. C is the north pole of the earth; D, its south pole; the line C D, the axis of the earth in perpendicular position, and coincident with the corresponding portion of the axis of the starry heavens. The space 1 1 1 1 is the abode of the supreme god or gods; 2, Europe; 3, Asia; 4, Libya, or the known portion of Africa; 5 5 5, the ocean, or "ocean stream"; 6 6 6, the abode of disembodied spirits and rulers of the dead; 7 7 7 7, the lowest hell.

Now, to make this key a graphic illustration of Homeric cosmology, it is only necessary to write in place of 1 1 1 1 "Lofty Olympos;" in place of 5 5 5, "The Ocean Stream;" in place of 6 6 6, "House of Aïdes" (Hades); and in place of 7 7 7 7, "Gloomy Tartaros." Imagine, then, the light as falling from the upper heavens — the lower terrestrial hemisphere, therefore, as forever in the shade; imagine the Tartarean abyss as filled with Stygian gloom and blackness — fit dungeon-house for dethroned gods and powers of evil; imagine the "men-illuminating" sun, the "well-tressed" moon, the "splendid" stars, silently wheeling round the central upright axis of the lighted hemispheres, — and suddenly the confusions and supposed contradictions of classic cosmology disappear. We are in the very world in which immortal Homer lived and sang. It is no longer an obscure crag in Thessaly, from which heaven-shaking Zeus proposes to suspend the whole earth and ocean. The eye measures for itself the nine days' fall of Hesiod's brazen anvil from heaven to earth, from earth to Tartarus. The Hyperboreans are now a possibility. Now a *descensus ad inferos* can be made by voyagers in the black ship. Unnumbered commentators upon Homer have professed their despair of ever being able to harmonize the passages in which Hades is represented as "beyond the ocean," with those in which it is represented as "subterranean." Conceive of man's dwelling-place, of Hades, and the ocean, as in this key, and the notable difficulty instantaneously vanishes. Interpreters of the Odyssey have found it impossible to understand how the westward and northward sailing voyager could suddenly be found in waters and amid islands unequivocally associated with the East. The present key explains it perfectly; showing, what no one seems heretofore to have suspected, that the voyage of Odysseus is a poetical account of an imaginary *circumnavigation of the mythical earth in the upper or northern hemisphere, including a trip to the southern or under hemisphere, and a visit to the ὀμφαλὸς θαλάσσης, or North Pole.*

The difficulties hitherto experienced in representing in a satisfactory manner the Yggdrasil of Norse mythology, the cosmical "fig-tree" of the Vedas, the "winged oak" of Pherecydes, etc., quite disappear when once, with understanding of the supposed true position of the universe in space, the centre line of the trunk of the tree is made coincident with the axis of the starry heavens.

In any chart or picture of the ancient Iranian cosmology, constructed according to this key, the Iranian Olympus, Harô berezaiti, will join the solid earth to heaven, while underneath, the mount of demons, dread Arezûra, will penetrate the nether darkness of the lowest hell. In Egyptian and Hindu cosmology the same opposed circumpolar projections of the earth are clearly traceable. To Harô berezaiti (Alborz) corresponds Mount Sar of ancient Egyptian mythology, the Kharsak Kurra of the Akkadians, the Har Moed of Babylonia (Isa. xiv. 13, 14), the Sumeru of the Hindus and Buddhists, the Asgard of the Northmen, the Pearl Mountain of the Chinese. The comparative study of those mythic mounts can leave no one in doubt as to the location of that heavenly height, where

> " the ever firm
> Seat of the gods is, by the winds unshaken,
> Nor ever wet with rain, nor ever showered
> With snow, but cloudless æther o'er it spreads,
> And glittering light encircles it around,
> On which the happy gods aye dwell in bliss."

In like manner, the comparative study of the myths of the ocean and of the under-worlds of ancient peoples leaves no room for doubt that these, too, were originally adjusted to a geocentric conception of the universe, and to an earth which was figured as a globe. With such a key the most perplexing cosmological problems, such as the origin of the strange concentric *dwîpas* of the Puranas, the origin and significance of the Sabean myth of Ur, the son of Rouhaïa, and many others, receive at once a plain and satisfactory solution.

Even the Kojiki, the most ancient of the sacred books of Japan, should have taught us to credit the early nations of the world with better knowledge of the earth than we have done; for in its beautiful cosmogony the earth revolves, and Izanagi's spear is only its upright axis.

---

As one out of a multitude of possible tests of the foregoing key, let us apply it to the interpretation of " the tall pillars of Atlas," which

γαῖάν τε καὶ οὐρανὸν ἀμφὶς ἔχουσιν.[1]

[1] *Odyssey*, I., 52-54.

In approaching the study of this subject several questions occur to every thoughtful beginner, the answers to which he can nowhere find.    For instance: How can Homer speak of the pillars of Atlas, using the plural, when elsewhere in the early Greek mythology the representations always point to only one?    Again, if there is but one, and that in the west, near the Gardens of the Hesperides,[1] what corresponding supports sustain the sky in the east, the north, and the south?    Or, if Atlas's pillar is only one of many similar ones supporting heaven around its whole periphery, how came it to be so much more famous than the rest?    Or, if Homer's plural indicates that all of them belonged to Atlas, how came the idea of one pillar to be so universally prevalent?    If the support of heaven was at many points, and at its outermost rim, how could Hesiod venture to represent the whole vault as poised on Atlas's head and hands?[2]    Again, if it is the special function of Atlas, or of his pillar, to stand on the solid earth and hold up the sky, he would seem to have no special connection with the sea: why, then, should Homer introduce the strange statement that Atlas "knows all the depths of the sea"?    This certainly seems very mysterious.    Again, if the office of the pillar or pillars is to prop up the sky, they

---

[1] Hesiod, *Theogony*, 517.    Atlas pflegt immer mit den Hesperiden genannt zu werden.    Preller, *Griechische Mythologie*, vol. i., p. 348.

[2] *Theogony*, 747.    Moreover, how could one limited being have charge of so many and so widely separated pillars?    "It can scarcely be doubted that the words ἀμφὶς ἔχουσιν, *Odyssey* I., 54, do not mean that these columns surround the earth; for in this case they must be not only many in number, but it would be obvious to the men of a myth-making and myth-speaking age, that a being stationed in one spot could not keep up, or hold, or guard, a number of pillars surrounding either a square or a circular earth." Cox, *Mythology of the Aryan Nations*.    London, 1870: vol. i., p. 37, *n.*

of course sustain different relations to earth and heaven.
They bear up the one, and are themselves borne up by
the other. Yet, singularly enough, Homer's *locus classicus*
places them in exactly the same relation to the two.[1]
Worse than this, Pausanias unqualifiedly and repeatedly
asserts that, according to the myth, Atlas supports upon
his shoulders "both earth and heaven."[2] And with this
corresponds the language of Æschylus.[3] But what sort of
a poetic imagination is this which represents a mighty
column as upholding not only a vast superincumbent
weight, but also, and at the same time, its own pedestal?
Is this a specimen creation of that immortal Hellenic
genius, which the whole modern world is taught almost to
adore?

Turning to the authorities in textual and mythological
interpretation, our beginner finds no help. On the con-
trary, their wild guesses and mutual contradictions only
confuse him more and more. Völcker tells him, with all
the assuring emphasis of leaded type, that "in Atlas is
given a personification of the art of navigation, the conquest
of the sea by means of human skill, by commerce, and the
gains of commerce."[4] Preller instructs him to reject this
view, and to think of this mysterious son of Iapetos as
a "sea-giant representing the upbearing and supporting

---

[1] "For that both heaven and earth are meant, not heaven alone, is
proved by various poetic passages, and by other testimonies." Preller,
*Griechische Mythologie*, vol. i., p. 348.

[2] Book V., 11, 2; 18, 1. One interpreter makes the profound suggestion
that in this passage the γῆν is "added by a zeugma"! Merry and Riddell,
*Odyssey*, I., 53.

[3] *Prometheus Bound*, 349, 425 *ff*.

[4] *Mythologie des japetischen Geschlechts*, p. 49 *ff*. Followed by K. O.
Müller, Keightley, Anthon, and many others.

almightiness of the ocean in contrast with the earth-shattering might of Poseidon."[1] The classical dictionaries only perplex him with multitudinous puerilities invented by ignorant Euhemeristic scholiasts, — stories to the effect that the original Atlas was merely the astronomer who first constructed an artificial globe to represent the sky; or that he was a North-west African, who, having ascended a lofty promontory the better to observe the heavenly bodies, fell off into the sea, and so gave name both to the mountain and to the Atlantic Ocean. Schoemann does not profess a positive and certain understanding of the matter, but suggests that the mysterious Titan was in all probability "originally a gigantic mountain-god" of some sort.[2]

Bryant at first makes Atlas a mountain supporting a temple or temple-cave, called *Co-el*, house of God, whence "the Cœlus of the Romans," vol. i., p. 274. In the next volume, however, he says that "under the name of Atlas is meant the Atlantians." And quoting "The Odyssey," he translates thus: " *They* [the Atlantians] *had also long pillars, or obelisks, which referred to the sea, and upon which was delineated the whole system both of heaven and earth;* ἀμφίς, *all around, both on the front of the obelisk and on the other sides.*"[3]

If our investigator asks, as did an ancient grammarian, how Atlas could stand on the earth and support heaven on his head, if heaven was so far removed that

[1] *Griechische Mythologie*, vol. i., 32, 348.  Followed by Faesi and others.
[2] G. F. Schoemann. *Die hesiodische Theogonie ausgelegt.*  Berlin, 1868, p. 207.
[3] Analysis of Ancient Mythology, London, 1807, vol. ii., 91.  The Italics are the author's.

an anvil would require nine days and nights in which
to fall through the distance, Paley kindly explains that
"the poet's notion doubtless was, that Atlas held up the
sky near its junction with earth in the far west."[1] In
this case, of course, a reasonably short giant would answer
the purpose. If, after all his consultations of authorities,
our youth is still unsatisfied, and to make a last effort for
light turns to the illustrious Welker, he learns as an
important final lesson, that when an ancient author says
"heaven and earth," it is not for a moment to be supposed
that he literally means "heaven and earth," and that, if
they had remembered this, writers on mythology would
have spared themselves "a vast amount of brain-racking
and ineffectual *pro*-and-*contra* pleading."[2] With this as
the sole outcome of all his researches, may not a beginner well despair of ever getting any knowledge of the
meaning of the myth, if, indeed, he can still imagine it to
have had a meaning?

Here, as everywhere, the truth at once explains and
removes all the difficulties which a false and groundless
presupposition has created.

Once conceive of the Homeric world as we have reconstructed it, and how clear and beautiful the conception
of the pillars of Atlas becomes! They are simply the

---

[1] *The Epics of Hesiod*, p. 229. On the other hand, another English interpreter would give us a giant with shoulders as broad as the whole heaven,
and translate ἀμφὶς ἔχουσιν "which support at either side; *i.e.*, at the East
and West." Merry and Riddell, *Odyssey*, I., 53.

[2] "Viel Kopfbrechens und vergeblichen Hin- und Herredens hat der
Ausdruck des Pausanias gemacht ἐπὶ τῶν ὤμων κατὰ τὰ λεγόμενα οὐρανόν τε ἀνέχει
καὶ γῆν, der auch bei dem Gemälde von Panänos (5, 11, 2) wiederkehrt:
οὐρανὸν καὶ γῆν ἀνέχων παρέστηκε, indem man οὐρανὸν καὶ γῆν buchstäblich ver-
stehen zu müssen glaubte." *Gr. Götterlehre*, vol. i., pp. 746, 747.

upright axes of earth and heaven. Viewed in their relation to earth and heaven respectively, they are two ; but viewed in reference to the universe as an undivided whole, they are one and the same. Being coincident, they are truly one, and yet they are ideally separable. Hence singular or plural designations are equally correct and equally fitting. Transpiercing the globe at the very "navel or centre of the sea," Atlas's pillar penetrates far deeper than any recess of the waters' bed, and he may well be said to "know the depths of the whole sea." Or this statement may have reference to that primordial sea in which his pillar was standing when the geogonic and cosmogonic process began. In this sense how appropriate and significant would it have been if applied to Izanagi![1]

Again, the association of Atlas with the Gardens of the Hesperides, so far from disproving our interpretation, actually affords new confirmation, since Æschylus, Pherecydes, and the oldest traditions locate the Hesperides themselves, not in the west, but in the extreme north, beyond the Rhiphæan Mountains, in the vicinity of the Hyperboreans.[2]  In fact, there are very strong reasons for

---

[1] Compare the Vedic statement: "He who knows the golden reed standing in the waters is the mysterious Prajapati." Muir, *Sanskrit Texts,* vol. iv., p. 21.  Garrett, *Classical Dictionary of India,* art. "Skambha." Still another explanation is suggested by the Rig-Veda, X., 149: "Savitri has established the earth by supports; Savitri has fixed the sky in unsupported space; Savitri, the son of the waters, knows the place where the ocean supported issued forth." Muir, *Sanskrit Texts,* vol. iv., p. 110 (comp. Ludwig's German version).  According to this, he would be conceived of as knowing the depths of the whole ocean, because its celestial springs are about his head, and its lowest depths at his feet.

[2] Preller, *Griechische Mythologie,* vol. ii., p. 149.  Völcker, *Mythologische Geographie,* pp. 133 ff.  Wolfgang Menzel, *Die vorchristliche Unsterblichkeitslehre,* vol. i., p. 98.  Accordingly "lost Atlantis" must be looked for,

believing that these Gardens of the Hesperides were nothing other than the starry gardens of the circumpolar sky; that, therefore, the Hesperides were called the "Daughters of Night," and that the great serpent which assisted the nymphs in watching "the golden apples" was none other than the constellation Draco, whose brilliant constituent *a*, the astronomer's Thuban, was, less than fifty centuries ago, the pole-star of our heaven.

Once more, our interpretation perfectly harmonizes the passages which represent Atlas as a heaven-supporter with those which represent him as equally supporting earth. More than this, it reveals the curious fact, that Homer's description of the tall pillars of Atlas identifies them with the axes of earth and heaven so unmistakably, that, in order to blunder into the common mistranslation of it, it was first necessary to invent, and get the lexicographers to adopt, a span-new special meaning for the words ἀμφὶς ἔχειν, — a meaning necessitated by no other passage in the whole body of Homeric Greek. Homer's beautifully explicit language is, —

> Ἔχει δέ τε κίονας αὐτὸς
> μακράς, αἳ γαῖάν τε καὶ οὐρανὸν ἀμφὶς ἔχουσιν.

"Who, of his own right, possesses the tall pillars *which have around them earth and heaven.*"[1] Nowhere in Homeric, if, indeed, in any ancient Greek, does the expression mean "*to prop asunder.*"[2]

not between Europe and America, but at the pole, whither all the oldest ethnic traditions point us for the cradle of the human race.

[1] Compare *Odyssey*, XV., 184.
[2] Buttmann (*Lexilogus*, English translation, 5th ed., pp. 94-104) is no more successful in showing such a meaning than are the older dictionary-makers.

Finally, as to the supposed difficulty of imagining a heaven-upholder so tall that it would take a brazen anvil nine days and nights to fall from his head to his feet, if Professor Paley had remembered Sandalfon, the Talmudic Atlas, he would hardly have thought it necessary to locate the Hesiodic one on the edge of the earth where the sky is low. Of Sandalfon, Rabbi Eliezer has said, "There is an angel who standeth on earth, and reacheth with his head to the door of heaven. It is taught in the Mishna that he is called Sandalfon; he exceedeth his companions as much in height as one can walk in five hundred years, and that he standeth behind the chariot [Charles's Wain] and twisteth or bindeth the garlands for his Creator." [1]

Atlas's pillar, then, is the axis of the world. It is the same pillar apostrophized in the Egyptian document known as the great Harris Magic Papyrus, in these unmistakable words: "O long column, which commences in the upper and in the lower heavens!" [2]  It is, with scarce a doubt, what the same ancient people in their Book of the Dead so happily styled "the spine of the earth." [3]  It is the Rig-Veda's *vieltragende Achse des unaufhaltsam sich drehenden, nie alternden, nie morschwerdenden, durch den Lauf der Zeiten nicht abgenutzten Weltrads, auf welchem* ALLE WESEN STEHEN. [4]  It is the umbrella-staff of Burmese cosmology, the churning-stick of India's gods and

---

[1] Eisenmenger, *Entdecktes Judenthum*, Bd. II., p. 402 (Eng. vol. ii., p. 97). In all ancient cosmologies "the door of heaven" is at the north pole. *Sacred Books of the East*, vol. i., pp. 36, 37.

[2] *Records of the Past*, vol. x., p. 152.

[3] Chap. cxlii.

[4] Rig-Veda, I., 164. Grassman and Ludwig.

demons. It is the trunk of every cosmical tree.[1] It is the Tái Kih of the Chinese universe; the tortoise-piercing (earth-piercing) arrow of the Mongolian heaven-god; the spear of Izanagi. It is the cord which the ancient Vedic bard saw stretched from one extremity of the universe to the other.[2] Is it not the Psalmist's " line " of the heavens which "is gone out through" the very "earth" and on "to the end of the world"? It is the Irminsul of the Germans, as expressly recognized by Grimm. It is the tower of Kronos. It is the Talmudic pillar which connects the Paradise celestial and the Paradise terrestrial.

---

The fuller illustration and vindication of this key to ancient cosmology, its application to different systems of mythology and mythical geography, and the systematic exposition of said systems in accordance with this new interpretation, are tasks reserved for future and fuller treatises. The studies already completed render it certain that every existing systematic exposition of classic mythology is to be supplanted. Equally interesting is the question of the adaptation of this reconstruction of ancient cosmology to throw light on early Hebrew conceptions of the world and of Sheol. And, if the ancestors of the most ancient peoples had so correct a conception of the figure of the earth, our leading " Historians of Culture " have yet a good deal to learn respecting the mental state and capacity of prehistoric men.

[1] Ludwig, in his version of the Veda, finds repeated occasion for the use of the expression " *Stengel der Welt.*"
[2] Rig-Veda, X., 129, 5.

# English Literature.

## Arnold's English Literature.

HISTORICAL AND CRITICAL: With an Appendix on English Metres, and Summaries of the different literary periods. By THOMAS ARNOLD, M.A., of University College, Oxford. American edition. Revised. 12mo. Cloth. 558 pages. Mailing price, $1.65 ; Introduction, $1.20 ; Exchange, 75 cts.

## Craik's English of Shakespeare.

Illustrated in a Philological Commentary on Julius Cæsar. By GEORGE L. CRAIK, Queen's College, Belfast. Edited from the third revised London edition by W. J. ROLFE, Cambridge, Mass. 16mo. Cloth. 386 pages. Mailing price, $1.00; Introduction, 90 cts.

## Carpenter's Anglo-Saxon Grammar and Reader.

An Introduction to the study of the Anglo-Saxon Language, comprising an Elementary Grammar and carefully graded Selections for Reading, followed by Explanatory Notes and a Vocabulary. By STEPHEN H. CARPENTER, late Professor of Rhetoric and English Literature in the University of Wisconsin. 12mo. Cloth. 212 pages. Mailing price, 80 cts. ; Introduction, 60 cts.

## Carpenter's English of the XIV. Century.

Illustrated by Notes, Grammatical and Philological, on Chaucer's Prologue and Knight's Tale. By STEPHEN H. CARPENTER, late Professor of Rhetoric and English Literature in the University of Wisconsin. 12mo. Cloth. 313 pages. Mailing price, $1.00; Introduction, 90 cts.

## Chaucer's Parlament of Foules.

A revised Text, with Literary and Grammatical Introduction, Notes, and a full Glossary. By T. R. LOUNSBURY, Professor of English in the Sheffield Scientific School of Yale College. 12mo. Cloth. 111 pages. Mailing price, 55 cts.; Introduction, 40 cts.

## The Harvard Edition of Shakespeare's Complete

*Works.* By HENRY N. HUDSON, LL.D., Author of the *Life, Art, and Characters of Shakespeare,* Editor of *School Shakespeare,* etc. In *Twenty Volumes;* duodecimo; two plays in each volume; also in *Ten Volumes* of four plays each.

RETAIL PRICES.

| | | | | | | |
|---|---|---|---|---|---|---|
| 20-vol. edition, cloth | . | . | . $25.00 | 10-vol. edition, cloth | . . | . $20.00 |
| half-morocco | . | . | . 55.00 | half-morocco | . . . | 40.00 |
| half-calf | . | . | . 55.00 | half-calf | . . . | . 40.00 |
| tree calf | . | . | . 90.00 | tree calf | . . . | . 60.00 |

HUDSON'S "LIFE, ART, AND CHARACTERS OF SHAKESPEARE" (2 vols.) are uniform in size and binding with THE HARVARD EDITION, and are included with it at a little more than the above prices.

☞ *Buyers should be careful in ordering not to confound the* **Harvard Shakespeare** *with an* **Old Edition** *made in 1851, and sold under another name.*

## Hudson's Life, Art, and Characters of Shake-

*speare.* In 2 vols. 12 mo. 969 pages. Uniform in size with "THE HARVARD SHAKESPEARE," and matches it in the following bindings: —

| | | | |
|---|---|---|---|
| Cloth | . . . . . . . | Retail Price, $4.00 per set. |
| Half-calf | . . . . . . | " " 8.00 " |
| Half-morocco | . . . . . | " " 8.00 " |
| Tree calf | . . . . . . | " " 12.00 " |

## Hudson's School Shakespeare.

Revised and Enlarged Editions of twenty-three Plays, printed from new electrotype plates. Carefully expurgated for use in Schools, Clubs, and Families, with Explanatory Notes at the bottom of the page, and Critical Notes at the end of each volume. By H. N. HUDSON, LL.D., late Professor of English Literature in Boston University, Editor of "*The Harvard Shakespeare,*" and, for more than thirty years, a Teacher of Shakespeare in the Schools. One play in each volume. Square 16mo. Varying in size from 128–253 pages. Mailing Price of each, Cloth, 60 cents; Paper, 45 cents. Introduction Price, Cloth, 45 cents; Paper, 33 cents. Exchange, Cloth, 38 cents; Paper, 26 cents.

## English in Schools.

By HENRY N. HUDSON, LL.D., Author of new *School Edition of Shakespeare's Plays,* Text-Books on *Bacon, Burke, Addison, Webster, Wordsworth, Burns, Coleridge,* etc., and of the *Classical English Reader.* Sq. 16mo. Paper. 131 pages. Mailing Price, 25 cts.

## Hudson's Three-Volume Shakespeare.

For Schools, Families, and Clubs. With Introductions and Notes of each Play. 12mo. Cloth. 636–678 pages per volume. Mailing price, per volume, $1.65 ; Introduction, $1.20.

## Expurgated Family Shakespeare.

By H. N. HUDSON, LL.D., Editor of *"Harvard Shakespeare," "Life, Art, and Characters of Shakespeare,"* etc. In 23 vols. Same edition as *The School Shakespeare* described on page 2. Retail Price, per set (in box), $16.

## Hudson's Text-Book of Poetry.

From Wordsworth, Coleridge, Burns, Beattie, Goldsmith, and Thomson. With Sketches of the Author's Lives, and instructive foot-notes, historical and explanatory. For use in Schools and Classes. By H. N. HUDSON, LL.D. 12mo. Cloth. 694 pages. Mailing price, $1.65; Introduction, $1.20.

## Hudson's Text-Book of Prose.

From Burke, Webster, and Bacon. With Sketches of the Authors' Lives, and foot-notes, historical and explanatory. By H. N. HUD-SON, LL.D. 12mo. Cloth. 636 pages. Mailing price, $1.65 ; Introduction, $1.20.

## Hudson's Pamphlet Selections Prose and Poetry.

Annotated. 12mo. Paper. Mailing price of each, 33 cts. ; Introduction price, 24 cts.

## Hudson's Classical English Reader.

For High Schools, Academies, and the upper grades of Grammar Schools. Containing selections from Bryant, Burke, Burns, Byron, Carlyle, Coleridge, Cowley, Cowper, Dana, Froude, Gladstone, Goldsmith, Gray, Helps, Herbert, Hooker, Hume, Irving, Keble, Lamb, Landor, Longfellow, Macaulay, Milton, Peabody, Scott, Shakespeare, Southey, Spenser, Talfourd, Taylor, Webster, Whittier, Wordsworth, and other standard authors. With explanatory and critical foot-notes. 12mo. Cloth. 425 pages. Mailing price, $1.25; Introduction, 90 cts.; Exchange, 50 cts.

## First Two Books of Milton's Paradise Lost; and

*Milton's Lycidas.* By HOMER B. SPRAGUE, Ph.D., Principal of Girls' High School, Boston. 12mo. Cloth. 198 pages. Mailing price, 60 cts.; Introduction, 45 cts.

## Six Selections from Irving's Sketch-Book.

With full notes, questions, etc., for home and school use. By HOMER B. SPRAGUE, Ph.D., and M. E. SCATES, of the Girls' High School, Boston. 12mo. Cloth. 126 pages. Mailing price, 45 cents; Introduction, 32 cents.

# English Grammar.

## Elementary Lessons in English.   Part First:

*"HOW TO SPEAK AND WRITE CORRECTLY."* By W. D. WHITNEY of Yale College, and Mrs. N. L. KNOX. 12mo. Cloth. 129 pages. Mailing price, 50 cts.; Introduction, 30 cts.; Exchange, 22 cts.

## The Teacher's Edition of Elementary Lessons

*in English.* To accompany PART I.: *"HOW TO SPEAK AND WRITE CORRECTLY."* Prepared by Mrs. N. L. KNOX. 12mo. Cloth. 323 pages. Mailing price, 80 cts.; Introduction price, 60 cts.

## Whitney's Essentials of English Grammar.

For the Use of High Schools, Academies, and the Upper Grades of Grammar Schools. By Professor W. D. WHITNEY of Yale College. 12mo. Cloth. 260 pages. Mailing price, $1.00; Introduction, 70 cts.; Exchange, 40 cts.

## Outlines of the Art of Expression.

A Treatise on English Composition and Rhetoric, designed especially for Academies, High Schools, and the Freshman Class in Colleges. By J. H. GILMORE, Professor of Logic, Rhetoric, and English in the University of Rochester, N.Y. 12mo. Cloth. 117 pages. Mailing Price, 65 cts.; Introduction, 48 cts.

## Bigsby's Elements of English Composition.

By BERNARD BIGSBY, Lecturer on the English Language. 18mo. 155 pages. Mailing Price, 35 cts.; Introduction, 28 cts.; Exchange, 20 cts.

# Latin Text-Books.

## Allen and Greenough's Latin Grammar.

Revised, Enlarged, and printed from new plates in 1877. A Latin Grammar for schools and colleges, founded on Comparative Grammar. By J. H. ALLEN, Lecturer at Harvard University, and J. B. GREENOUGH, Professor of Latin at Harvard University. 12mo. Half morocco. 329 pages. With new and greatly-enlarged Index. Mailing price, $1.25 ; Introduction, 90 cts.; Exchange, 50 cts.

## Leighton's Latin Lessons.

Prepared to accompany Allen and Greenough's Latin Grammar. Containing also references to the Grammars of Andrews and Stoddard, Harkness, and Gildersleeve. By R. F. LEIGHTON, Ph.D. (Lips.), Principal of the Brooklyn (N.Y.) High School. Revised edition, with full Vocabularies prepared by R. F. Pennell. 12mo. Half morocco. 494 pages. Mailing Price, $1.25 ; Introduction, 90 cts.; Exchange, 50 cts.

## New Latin Method.

A Manual of Instruction in Latin, on the basis of a Latin Method prepared by J. H. ALLEN and J. B. GREENOUGH. 12mo. Cloth. 303 pages. Mailing Price, $1.00; Introduction, 70 cts. ; Exchange, 45 cts.

## Six Weeks' Preparation for Reading Cæsar.

With References to Allen and Greenough's, Gildersleeve's, and Harkness's Grammars. Designed to accompany a Grammar, and to prepare pupils for reading at sight. By JAMES M. WHITON. 18mo. Cloth. 75 pages. Mailing Price, 40 cts.; Introduction, 28 cts.

## Allen's Introduction to Latin Composition.

Revised and Enlarged, with references to the Grammars of Allen and Greenough, Gildersleeve, and Harkness. By WILLIAM F. ALLEN, Professor in the University of Wisconsin. With the coöperation of John Tetlow, A.M., Master of the Girls' Latin School, Boston, and Prof. Tracy Peck of Yale College. 12mo. Cloth. 181 pages. Mailing Price, $1.00 ; Introduction, 70 cts.; Exchange, 50 cts.

## Allen and Greenough's Latin Composition.

An Elementary Guide to Writing in Latin. Part I., Constructions of Syntax ; Part II., Exercises in Translation. 12mo. Cloth. 198 pages. Mailing Price, $1.25 ; Introduction, 90 cts.; Exchange, 50 cts.

## Allen and Greenough's Cæsar.

Cæsar's Gallic War: Four Books. With Historical Introduction, Notes, and a copperplate Map of Gaul. Also a full Vocabulary by R. F. PENNELL, of Phillips Exeter Academy. 12mo. Half morocco. 282 pages. Mailing Price, $1.10 ; Introduction, 80 cts.; Exchange, 50 cts.

## Allen and Greenough's Sallust.

The Conspiracy of Catiline as related by Sallust. With Introduction and Notes, explanatory and historical. 12mo. Cloth. 84 pages. Mailing Price, 65 cts.; Introduction, 45 cts.

## Allen and Greenough's Cicero.

**Thirteen Orations of Cicero,** chronologically arranged, covering the entire period of his public life. From the text of Baiter and Kayser. With Life, general and special Introductions, and Index of topics discussed. 12mo. Half morocco. 394 pages. Mailing Price, $1.25 ; Introduction, 90 cts.; Exchange, 50 cts.

**Eight Orations.** With Vocabulary by R. F. PENNELL. Mailing Price, $1.25 ; Introduction, 90 cts.; Exchange, 50 cts.

## Allen and Greenough's Preparatory Course of

*Latin Prose.* Containing Four Books of Cæsar's Gallic War, and Eight Orations of Cicero. With Vocabulary by R. F. PENNELL. 12mo. Half morocco. 518 pages. Mailing Price, $1.55 ; Introduction, $1.12; Exchange, 75 cts.

## Allen and Greenough's Virgil.

Containing the Pastoral Poems (*Bucolics*) and Six Books of the Æneid. Chiefly from the text of Ribbeck, with select various Readings, Introductions, Notes, and Index of Plants (compiled chiefly from Feé's *Flore de Virgile*, contained in Lemaire's "Bibliotheca Classica Latina "). 12mo. Half morocco. 372 pages.

**With Vocabulary:** Mailing Price, $1.55 ; Introduction, $1.12; Exchange, 75 cts.

**Without Vocabulary:** Mailing Price, $1.25 ; Introduction, 90 cts.; Exchange, 50 cts.

## Allen and Greenough's De Senectute.

Cicero's Dialogue on Old Age. With Introduction (on the adoption in Rome of the Greek philosophy) and Notes. 12mo. Cloth. 57 pages. Mailing Price, 55 cts.; Introduction, 40 cts.

## Auxilia Vergiliana ; or, First Steps in Latin Prosody.

By J. M. WHITON, Ph.D. 12mo. Paper cover. Mailing Price, 22 cts.; Introduction, 16 cts.

## Allen and Greenough's Ovid.

Selections from the Poems of Ovid, chiefly the Metamorphoses. Over 5,000 lines. With special Introductions, Notes, and Index of Proper Names. 12mo. Half morocco. 282 pages.
    With Vocabulary : Mailing Price, $1.55 ; Introduction, $1.12 ; Exchange, 75 cts.
    Without Vocabulary : Mailing Price, $1.25 ; Introduction, 90 cts.; Exchange, 50 cts.

## Greenough's Virgil. Vol. I.

Containing the Pastoral Poems (*Bucolics*) and Six Books of the Æneid. With Life of the Poet, Introductions, a Synopsis preceding each Book, and an Index of Plants. Also 123 Illustrations from ancient objects of art. Fully annotated, for School and College Use, by J. B. GREENOUGH of Harvard University.
    The text follows Ribbeck in the main, variations being noted in the margin ; and the references are to Allen and Greenough's, Gildersleeve's, and Harkness's Latin Grammars. 12mo. Cloth. 467 pages.
    With Vocabulary: Mailing Price, $1.55; Introduction, $1.12; Exchange, 75 cts.
    Without Vocabulary: Mailing Price, $1.25 ; Introduction, 90 cts.; Exchange, 50 cts.

## Greenough's Virgil. Vol. II.

Containing the last six Books of the Æneid and the *Georgics.* Chiefly from the text of Ribbeck, with select various Readings, Introductions, and Notes. By J. B. GREENOUGH, Harvard University. 12mo. Cloth.
    *[In preparation.*

## Allen's Latin Primer.

A First Book of Latin for Boys and Girls. By J. H. ALLEN. 12mo. Cloth. 181 pages. Mailing Price, $1.00; Introduction, 70 cts.; Exchange, 45 cts.

## Allen's Latin Reader.

Consisting of Selections from Cæsar (the invasion of Britain, and account of the Gallic and German populations), Curtius (Anecdotes of Alexander), Nepos (Life of Hannibal), Sallust (Jugurtha, abridged), Ovid, Virgil, Plautus, and Terence (single scenes), Cicero and Pliny (Letters), and Tacitus (the Conflagration of Rome). With Notes and General Vocabulary. 12mo. Half morocco. 532 pages. Mailing Price, $1.55; Introduction, $1.12; Exchange, 75 cts.

## Allen's Latin Lexicon.

A General Vocabulary of Latin, with Supplementary Tables of Dates, Antiquities, &c. By J. H. ALLEN. 12mo. Cloth. 214 pages. Mailing Price, $1.00; Introduction, 70 cts.; Exchange, 45 cts.

## Germania and Agricola of Tacitus.

Edited, for School and College Use, by W. F. ALLEN, Professor of Latin in the University of Wisconsin. 12mo. Cloth. 142 pages. Mailing Price, $1.10; Introduction, $1.00.

## King's Latin Pronunciation.

A Brief Outline of the Roman, Continental, and English Methods, by D. B. KING, Adjunct Professor of Latin in Lafayette College. 12mo. Cloth. 24 pages. Mailing Price, 25 cts.; Introduction Price, 20 cts.

## Remnants of Early Latin.

Chiefly inscriptions. Selected and Explained, for use in Colleges, by FREDERICK D. ALLEN, Professor of Classical Philology, Harvard College. Square 16mo. 106 pages. Mailing Price, 80 cts.; Introduction, 75 cts.

## Cicero De Natura Deorum.

LIBRI TRES, with the commentary of G. F. Schoemann, translated and edited by AUSTIN STICKNEY. 12mo. Cloth. 348 pages. Mailing Price, $1.55; Introduction, $1.40.

## Selections from the Latin Poets.

Catullus, Lucretius, Tibullus, Propertius, Ovid, and Lucan. With notes for Colleges. Edited by E. P. CROWELL, Professor of Latin, Amherst College. 12mo. Cloth. 300 pages. Mailing Price, $1.55; Introduction, $1.40.

## A Brief History of Roman Literature.

For Schools and Colleges. Translated and edited from the German edition of Bender by Professors E. P. CROWELL and H. B. RICHARDSON of Amherst College. Square 16mo. 152 pages. Mailing Price, $1.10; Introduction, 80 cts.

## An Etymology of Latin and Greek.

With a Preliminary Statement of the New System of Indo-European Phonetics, and Suggestions in Regard to the Study of Etymology. By CHARLES S. HALSEY, A.M., Principal of Union College Classical Institute, Schenectady, N.Y. 12mo. Cloth. 272 pages. Mailing Price, $1.55; Introduction, $1.40.

## Madvig's Latin Grammar.

Carefully revised by THOMAS A. THACHER, Professor of Latin, Yale College. 12mo. Half morocco. 515 pages. Mailing Price, $2.50; Introduction, $1.50.

## The Latin Verb.

Illustrated by the Sanskrit. By C. H. PARKHURST, formerly of Williston Seminary. 12mo. Cloth. 55 pages. Mailing Price, 40 cts.; Introduction, 35 cts.

## Ginn & Heath's Classical Atlas.

By A. KEITH JOHNSTON, LL.D., F.R.G.S., aided by W. E. GLADSTONE, Prime Minister of England. Bound in full cloth, with guards, similar to Long's Classical Atlas (7½ × 12 inches). Also bound in strong boards, cloth back, (15 × 12 inches). Mailing Price, **Cloth**, $1.75; **Boards**, $1.30. Introduction, **Cloth**, $1.40; **Boards**, $1.05.

## Classical Wall-Maps.

Engraved by W. & A. K. JOHNSTON, Edinburgh. Price, express paid, $5.00 each; Introduction Price, $4.00 each; Introduction Price of three or more, $3.50 each.

## White's Junior Student's Latin Lexicons.

**LATIN-ENGLISH.** Morocco. Mailing Price, $2.20; Introduction, $1.80. Sheep. Mailing Price, $2.50; Introduction, $2.00.
**LATIN-ENGLISH and ENGLISH-LATIN.** Sheep. Mailing Price, $3.30; Introduction, $2.70.
**ENGLISH-LATIN.** Sheep. Mailing Price, $1.90; Introduction, $1.60.

# Greek Text-Books.

## Goodwin's Greek Grammar.

By WILLIAM W. GOODWIN, Ph.D., Eliot Professor of Greek Literature
in Harvard College. Revised and Enlarged Edition. Published in
December, 1879. 12mo. Half morocco. 425 pages. Mailing Price,
$1.65; Introduction, $1.20; Exchange, 90 cts.

## White's First Lessons in Greek.

*Revised and Enlarged Edition.* ..Prepared "to accompany Goodwin's
Greek Grammar, and designed as an introduction either to his Greek
Reader or to his Selections from Xenophon and Herodotus, or to the
Anabasis of Xenophon. With a Companion Pamphlet of Parallel
References to Hadley's *Greek Grammar*. By JOHN WILLIAMS
WHITE, Ph.D., Assistant Professor of Greek in Harvard University.
12mo. Half morocco. Mailing Price, $1.30; Introduction, 94 cts.;
Exchange, 70 cts.

## Leighton's New Greek Lessons.

With references to Hadley's Greek Grammar as well as to Goodwin's
New Greek Grammar. Intended as an introduction to Xenophon's
Anabasis or to Goodwin's Greek Reader. By R. F. LEIGHTON, Ph.D.
(Lips.), Principal Brooklyn High School, N.Y. 12mo. Half morocco.
Mailing Price, $1.30; Introduction, 94 cts.; Exchange, 70 cts.

## First Four Books of Xenophon's Anabasis.

With an illustrated Vocabulary. Edited by Professors W. W. GOODWIN
and JOHN WILLIAMS WHITE of Harvard University. 12mo. Half
morocco. 355 pages. Mailing Price, $1.65; Introduction, $1.20;
Exchange, 90 cts.
  **Without Vocabulary.** Mailing Price, $1.10; Introduction, 75 cts.;
Exchange, 50 cts.

## Goodwin's Greek Reader.

Consisting of Selections from Xenophon, Plato, Herodotus, and
Thucydides; being the full amount of Greek Prose required for
admission to Harvard University. With Colored Maps, Notes, and
References to the revised and enlarged edition of Goodwin's Greek
Grammar. Edited by Professor W. W. GOODWIN of Harvard Uni-
versity. 12mo. Half morocco. 384 pages. Mailing price, $1.65;
Introduction, $1.20; Exchange, 90 cts.

## Goodwin's Greek Moods and Tenses.

By WILLIAM W. GOODWIN, Ph.D., Eliot Professor of Greek Literature in Harvard University. Seventh Edition. Revised and Enlarged. 12mo. Cloth. 279 pages. Mailing Price, $1.65; Introduction, $1.50.

## Essential Uses of the Moods in Greek and Latin.

Prepared by R. P. KEEP, Ph.D., Instructor in the Classical Department of Williston Seminary, at Easthampton, Mass. Square 16mo. Mailing Price, 40 cts.; Introduction, 28 cts.

## Sidgwick's Greek Prose Composition.

By ARTHUR SIDGWICK, Lecturer at Corpus Christi College, Oxford, and Fellow of Trinity College, Cambridge. 12mo. Cloth. 280 pages. Mailing Price, $1.65; Introduction, $1.33.

## Philippics of Demosthenes.

Contains the First, Second, and Third Philippics, with an Introduction and Explanatory Notes. With references to Goodwin's and Hadley's Greek Grammars. By FRANK B. TARBELL, Yale College. 12mo. Cloth. 138 pages. Mailing Price, $1.10; Introduction Price, $1.00.

## Hellenic Orations of Demosthenes.

*Symmories*, *Megalopolitans*, and *Rhodians*. With revised text and commentary by ISAAC FLAGG, Ph.D., Professor of Greek in Cornell University. 12mo. 103 pages. Mailing price, $1.10; Introduction Price, $1.00.

## Medea of Euripides.

Edited, with Notes and an Introduction, by FREDERICK D. ALLEN, Ph.D., Professor of Classical Philology in Harvard University. 12mo. Cloth. 141 pages. Mailing Price, $1.10; Introduction, $1.00.

## Œdipus Tyrannus of Sophocles.

Edited, with an Introduction, Notes, and full Explanation of the Metres, by JOHN WILLIAMS WHITE, Ph.D., Assistant Professor of Greek in Harvard University. 12mo. Cloth. 219 pages. Mailing Price, $1.25; Introduction, $1.12.

## *Orations of Lysias.*

With Biographical Introduction, Notes, and Table of Various Readings. Edited by JAMES MORRIS WHITON, Ph.D. 12mo. Mailing Price, $1.10; Introduction, $1.00.

## *Selections from the Greek Lyric Poets.*

With an Historical Introduction, giving a brief survey of the development of Greek Poetry until the time of Pindar, and also Notes for the student's use. By HENRY M. TYLER, Professor of Greek and Latin in Smith College. 12mo. Cloth. 184 pages. Mailing Price, $1.10; Introduction, $1.00.

## *Selected Odes of Pindar.*

With Notes and an Introduction by THOMAS D. SEYMOUR, Professor of the Greek Language and Literature in Yale College. The text is that of Bergk's fourth edition, and the metrical schemes are according to Schmidt's "Kunstformen der Griechischen Poesie." 12mo. Cloth. 300 pages. Mailing Price, $1.55; Introduction, $1.40.

## *Stein's Summary of the Dialect of Herodotus.*

Translated by Professor JOHN WILLIAMS WHITE, Ph.D., from the German of the fourth edition of Herodotus by Heinrich Stein. Paper, 15 pages. Mailing Price, 10 cts.; Introduction Price, 10 cts.

## *Schmidt's Rhythmic and Metric of the Clas-*

*sical Languages.* Edited from the German by JOHN WILLIAMS WHITE, Ph.D., Assistant Professor of Greek in Harvard University. Designed as a Manual for Classes in the Greek and Latin Poets. 8vo. Cloth. 204 pages. Mailing Price, $2.65; Introduction, $2.50.

## *Liddell and Scott's Greek-English Lexicon.*

The sixth and last Oxford Edition, unabridged. 4to. Sheep. 1,881 pages. Mailing Price, $10.00; Introduction, $7.50 net.

## *Liddell and Scott's Greek-English Lexicon.*

ABRIDGED from the last Oxford Edition of the unabridged (see above), and carefully revised throughout. With Appendix of Proper and Geographical Names, by J. M. WHITON. Square 12mo. 835 pages. Morocco back. Mailing Price, $1.00; Introduction, $1.50 net.

www.ingramcontent.com/pod-product-compliance
Lightning Source LLC
Chambersburg PA
CBHW021457090426
42739CB00009B/1758